Other Poetry Collections By Sandra de Helen
From Launch Point Press

Lesbian Humor is Not an Oxymoron: Light Verse by Sandra de Helen

Desire Returns for a Visit: Intimate Poems about Lesbian Love

Praise for the Poetry of Sandra de Helen

Desire Returns for a Visit

"[Sandra de Helen's] book of poems is a great way to read a truthful, witty, poignant memoir about lesbian love."
~Judy Grahn, Ph.D., poet, writer, trailblazer

"I didn't need to read beyond the first line of the first poem in Sandra de Helen's collection *Desire Returns* to know I'd be loving this book: "Wearing makeup is as unnecessary as / painting crickets." What a fanciful imagination. What a cohesive, splendidly ordered body of work.

It's not often I find poems that speak so directly of and to my lesbian heart. Love poems all, even when love kicks and confuses, this poet portrays the lesbian core."
~Lee Lynch, novelist, essayist, short story writer, trailblazer

"This book covers the breadth and depth of a relationship from its exciting beginning to its ending."
~Jazzy Mitchell, author of *Undertow* and many other novels

"From the opening poem to the last 'Dead Reckoning' I found this collection of poetry to be very accessible. In this hectic world where my to do list is a page long, and like Sisyphus never ending, I found myself reading one poem then going on to read several more, doing this over the course of a couple weeks… Many of the titles open with a poem by Emily Dickinson and follow with a response from de Helen's own work. This is a lovely gift."
~E. B. Mulligan, Vine Voice

"These are fresh poems in every sense of the word. Flirty, audacious, original. A fresh take on Dickinson's love of women and words. A brazen exploration of the life cycle of love affairs. This book is an open-mouthed kiss to the reader. It will leave you breathless."
~**G.L. Morrison, poet, lover of words, and short fiction writer**

"The author wrote with lyrical, beautiful sentences that painted pictures in my mind. Her choices in style and presentation were fabulous."
~**Rainbow Awards Judge, Honorable Mention**

Lesbian Humor is Not an Oxymoron

"Irreverent while still relevant. Poignant, pungent, playfully pugnacious and peppered with poultry. Sandra de Helen's light verse (which includes letters to Santa and martians) illuminates the silliest corners of her skylarking sapphist psyche."
~**G.L. Morrison, poet, lover of words, and short fiction writer**

"The author isn't kidding that Lesbian Humor is Not an Oxymoron. This book is full of zingers: 'I leaned in for a kiss. She offered me a peppermint.' 'My friend John, a holdover from the union of older men who trained hard to be curmudgeons …'I gave the damned boots away. They were kicking my ass.' 'But you know that world famous Golden Gate? It's orange.' (Just to name a few.) 5.0 out of 5 stars "
~**Kate Kasten,Award-winning author of plays, short stories, essays, and books**

Poetry for the New Millennium ~ Volume III

POETRY FOR THE PEOPLE!
Heavy Verse

by

Sandra de Helen

2020

POETRY FOR THE PEOPLE is a work of poetic fiction. Names, characters, places, and incidents are either the product of the author's imagination or are used fictitiously. Any resemblance to actual persons living or dead, business establishments, events, or locales is entirely coincidental. Further copyright notes can be found at the conclusion of the collection.

A Launch Point Press Trade Paperback Original

Copyright © 2020 by Sandra de Helen

All rights reserved. Launch Point Press supports copyright which enables creativity, free speech, and fairness. Thank you for buying the authorized version of this book and for following copyright laws by not using or reproducing any part of this book in any manner whatsoever, including Internet usage, without written permission from Launch Point Press, except in the form of brief quotations embodied in critical reviews and articles. Your cooperation and respect supports authors and allows Launch Point Press to continue to publish the books you want to read.

ISBN: 978-1-63304-034-2

FIRST EDITION: First Printing, 2020

Editing: Lori L. Lake
Formatting: Patty Schramm
Cover Design: Lorelei

Portland, Oregon
www.LaunchPointPress.com

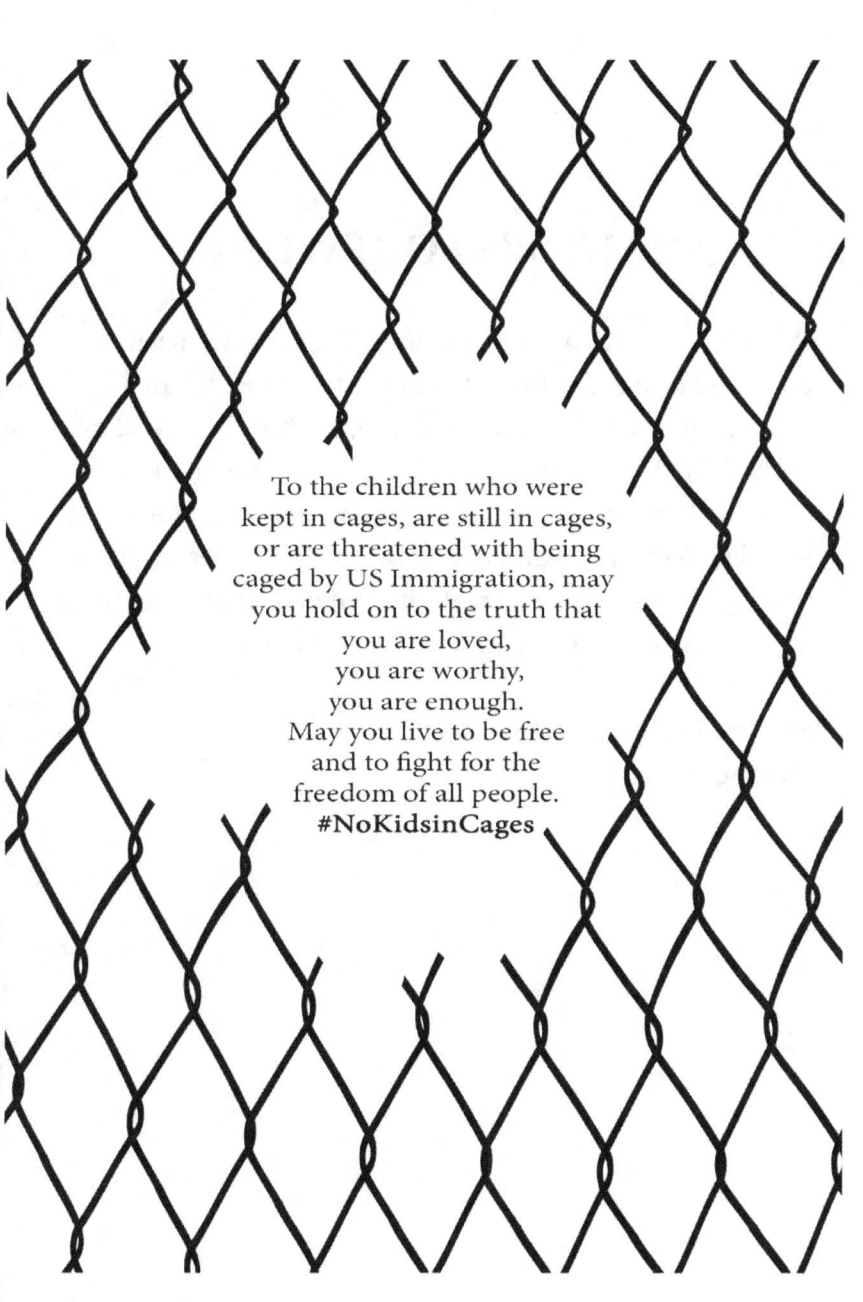

AUTHOR'S FOREWORD

Whether by nature or nurture, I've always been a political animal. I refused to eat meat when I learned it came from animals. I was a feminist before I knew the term. My first published work was a poem about abortion (the need for) when I was fourteen and abortion was illegal in this country. I chose women's theater and writing as my greatest creativity outlets. These poems show the wide range of topics that inspire me.

Sandra de Helen
October, 2020

CONTENTS

DEDICATION
AUTHOR'S FOREWORD

INTRO
1   Where You From

SOCIAL JUSTICE
3   Abandoned
4   Cash Poor
5   Message from a Caged Child
6   Flaming Trees
7   The Loss of Bees
8   Message from a Caged Animal
9   Note to Teenage Women
11   Every Woman
13   Marching Madness
14   Democratic Debate 2016
15   My Country's Wardrobe
16   Publicity Shoot
18   Take Back the Night
19   Manhattan 1979: A Prose Poem
21   Divided We Fall

WAR AND PEACE
23   Foreboding
24   Hiroshima Stories
25   A-Bomb

26	Shadows of War
28	White Sands
29	Black Gold
31	Nine-Eleven
32	Even the Evil Deserve to Rest in Peace
34	Poem to 45: you don't deserve a capital Y
36	Margaret Nin to Husband Johann Faust, 1597
37	Time Out for Peace

THE PERSONAL IS POLITICAL

39	Schlitz! A Drinking Song
40	Disney Revolution
42	Vegetarian Now
44	Rabbit
45	Sole/Soul
46	Diving In
48	The Right Foundation
50	Be a Hairy Woman
51	Abundance
53	Politics and Betrayal
55	Point/Counterpoint
56	The Joys of Working
57	The Duel
58	Here, Bury This
59	Can You Hear Me Now?
61	To Each His Own

CELEBRITY POLITICS
63   Emancipation
65   A Message to Gloria Steinem
66   Elegy for Lanford Wilson
67   Hef, circa 2012
68   Goodbye, Hugh. Seriously

POET WARRIORS AT WORK
71   Poet Warriors
72   Deed
73   Disruptive/new self
75   First Assignment: Extreme Heat Season
77   Civil Rights: Next Phase

HOME ISOLATION DAYS
79   Day 66: A WWII Moon
80   Day 76: No End
82   Day 82: Can I Change?
83   Day 100: The First 100
85   Day 101: Tulsa Rally
86   Day 110: Covid Dreams
87   Day 112: Happy July
88   Day 115: Pointless Fireworks
90   Day 120: Natural Hugs
92   Day 131: Living in the Now
94   Day 174: Fierce Feminist vs. Fly Catcher: Debates 2020

OUTRO
97   Today's the Day

AFTERWORD
ACKNOWLEDGMENTS
ABOUT THE POET

"Sometimes we are blessed with being able to choose the time, and the arena, and the manner of our revolution, but more usually we must do battle where we are standing."

~Audre Lorde

INTRO

Where You From

I'm from Helen, Maggie, Lucinda
Women who worked.
I'm from factories, and farming, and taking in laundry
I'm from the hills of Missouri.
The Ozarks.

I'm from wanting an education,
learning any way I can.
I'm from resourcefulness. Making my own
soap, clothes, growing and canning
beans, tomatoes, potatoes, all manner of fruit.

I'm from reading, writing, and arithmetic.
I'm from memorizing poetry and speeches.
I'm from pinching pennies and making do.
I'm from flour sacks and catalog pictures.
Wish books.

I'm from dreamers and poets and women
with calluses. I'm from hard scrabble
and hard nights. I'm from the rubble
we call stardust. Just like you.

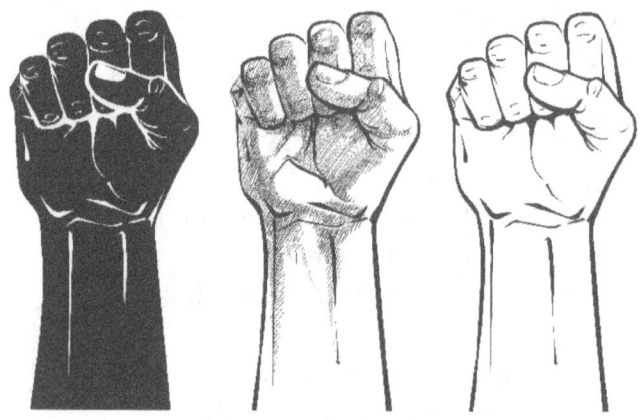

SOCIAL JUSTICE

Abandoned

People need shelter – they
build a home. Simple or grand,
well-constructed, it will welcome
occupants for hundreds of years.

Until abandoned by black death,
or war, or the end of the family line.

An empty house cannot stand
for long. Floors fall away at the touch of a shadow
one day after the roof caves in from the
last straw blown across by a summer
wind.

Entropy sets in and the secrets
left behind will not support
the walls. While the cornerstones gather
moss, dirt settles the arguments
holding grudges in opposite corners.

Cash Poor

You asked how not to be broke.
The answer is simple: be born rich

and spend it all. Otherwise,
you are screwed. Wages

are low, prices are high, no one
gets a raise, and you're lucky

to have a job in the first place.
Cash poor? Get used to it. It could

be worse. Broke just means
waiting for your next paycheck. You

could be flat-assed busted. That's when
you don't have a job. Or any

prospect of a job. You could
be houseless. You could be begging

for your next meal. You should be
grateful your problem is negative cash flow.

Message from a Caged Child

I am locked up, waiting to learn
how long. When will I see my
people again? Why did they
leave me here? Where did they go?

I need more food, more water,
a bath. This silver paper is not
a blanket, and I am cold.

Other kids speak, but I don't
understand them. Grown-ups
stand in corners, never looking
in my eyes. I talk to myself.

Yesterday I cried out loud.
Today my tears fall without sound.
I screamed when they took me
from my mother. She let them
take me. I will never scream again.

Flaming Trees

In Missouri, fragrant sumac blooms today
signal the beginning of the peak of fall
color. Most of the country is hosting these

rooted fireworks, spreading the magical
flames from the Atlantic to the Pacific
oceans. Only a few states are spared this

prestidigitation. In southern California, our
fires come with smoke, panic, and terrible
consequences. Without indecision, we fight

them with everything we have. The death
toll climbs weekly. We lose all manner of
sentient beings, millions of acres of life.

We have no time to mourn the lack of
deciduous entertainers.

The Loss of Bees

More than slightly bereft today as
colony collapse disorder once again

reported on the rise – could be
cellphones or perhaps pesticides

malnutrition, GMOs, radiation
migration, even incest – but years

after we first noticed it, humans
prefer to call it a mystery.

Message from a Caged Animal

I have been locked up for years waiting for
the one who will unlock the door and release me

to my original habitat. The animals in lab coats have
tested me for HIV, AIDS, and cut out half my

brain to see whether I could still function. They take
my blood and other fluids as quickly as I can produce

them. They've removed so many body parts my
kibble seems to rattle around inside me. I've run

mazes, worked puzzles, learned sign language, and
was put in a room once with 99 others and 100

typewriters to see what we were capable of
writing. I wrote about how to escape this cage.

Note to Teenage Women

Young men will show up with
their curls and sparkling eyes and
endearing terms. They will have strong

arms that remind you of the father
you always wished you had or
once had, but lost along the way

like that little red purse
you can't stop dreaming about.
Your own body will betray

you with desires and growth
or non-growth in places
where you most or least wish

for notice from your peers
and elders in your life.
Other young women will use cruel

words to describe your beautiful body
parts and the characteristics you
secretly treasure about yourself.

Ignore them.
What you must listen to
instead is the small voice deep

inside you. You may have to strain
for the next several
years in order to hear it.

Listen anyway. You will hear words
of encouragement, warning bells,

and calls to action. They will ring
out until you have the courage and
confidence to speak for yourself,
to join the rising chorus.

Every Woman

With one arm the woman holds
up her piece of the sky. With the
other arm she is fending off the
sexual advances of the man who
holds up his piece of the sky with
one hand and gropes female parts
with the other. Not every man, you
say. Let us be generous. Let's say
fifty percent of the men are groping
one hundred percent of the women.

Some men are vicious and violent
and grab women by the pussy. Or
worse. They masturbate themselves
while making women watch. They
rape women. They rape children.
They are the bad apples who give
all men a bad name. They are the
men who ensure that women
never feel safe.

In this age of micro-aggressions, we
see have come to see that women—
even women who have never been
harassed, molested, or raped—walk
to their cars looking over their
shoulders, keys sorted between their
fingers, fingers wrapped into a fist.
They lock their doors, they check

their surroundings, they quake in
fear when they walk into a darkened
parking garage.

Women rarely walk into alleys, but
if they do, they know they are risking
their lives.

Women carry their cocktails into the
restroom, choosing germs over possible
roofies.

When women express joy over the
birth of a son, they have to ask themselves
why they prefer a boy over a girl. If they
look to their own lives, they see the
shadow of fear that accompanies the
lives of girls. Boys are easier, they say.

If the world is to change, if women are
to be safe from men who grope, then men
who are not harassing, not molesting,
not raping, those men must help the
sky fall on the men who are.

Every woman deserves to live in
the same, safe world as every man.

Marching Madness

Much madness is divinest sense
To a discerning eye;
Much sense the starkest madness.
'T is the majority
In this, as all, prevails.
Assent, and you are sane;
Demur, -- you're straightway dangerous,
And handled with a chain.
~Emily Dickinson

Am I deluded? Or is the majority of the population irrational? It seems to me that all the spiritual leaders of the ages have espoused peace, forgiveness, asked us to do unto others as we prefer they do to us.

And yet, war rages across the globe. Racism, sexism, fat-ism prevail. Studies always show the majority practice one sort of spirituality or religion. Why are the believers not following the advice of the founders?

In loving my neighbor, protesting war, protesting injustice, marching like mad for peace, I join multitudes of others who do so. We are the minority. Which of us has lost our minds?

Democratic Debate 2016

Has everything gone haywire? We rush through
the day with one destination in mind: tonight's
debates by the candidates for head of state.

I attempt a mindful path, gazing at the overhead
sky, breathing deep. All around me the buzz.
I feel the excitement in the air as electricity.

Can you hear the crackling? Soon the debaters
will take their places. A gavel will fall. Questions
will arise and never be answered, as each

contender battles to make her point, tries to
win our vote. Still, we watch. As hopeful as
a hound waiting for a crumb to drop.

Some wait for a gaffe. Others like me
hope to be swept away in the rhetoric,
to hear answers to the questions

I hardly dare ask. My imagination goes wild as
I wait for the appointed hour.

My Country's Wardrobe

My country need not change her gown,
Her triple suit as sweet
As when 't was cut at Lexington,
And first pronounced "a fit."
Great Britain disapproves "the stars;"
Disparagement discreet, --
There's something in their attitude
~Emily Dickinson

My country needs to change her gown
her triple suit has grown rough – and

my country has grown too big for her
britches. The stars no longer shine

so brightly as they once did, some have
tarnished, turning against their own

citizens, forgetting everything – it seems.
Time for a refreshing shower, a renewal,

something softer, more colorful. Perhaps
all the hues of the rainbow?

Publicity Shoot

Two more university shootings today. Will the
shooters receive the publicity they seek?

Each one killed only one, though they injured more.
Big fail for both of the gunmen. Mass shootings
are not mass, until four persons have died.

Meanwhile, Republican presidential candidate
Ben Carson, a brain surgeon, is making an
ass of himself

by explaining how and why
gunshot victims could avoid being shot by
simply using their charisma to rally

all the victims to rush the shooter. Perhaps this
tactic could be included in freshman
orientation at all colleges and universities.

But wait, what about the kindergarteners and
everyone else who isn't currently enrolled in
higher education?

Dr. Carson has a cure for that as well:
train kindergarten teachers in diversionary tactics
and give them weapons.

As for the rest of us, didn't we see the movie
Die Hard? Rent it on Netflix if you haven't.

Whatever you do, be prepared.

Don't be afraid of guns, they don't kill people. Only people kill people.

As for me, I plan to stay away from people. Especially if they have guns.

Take Back the Night

Feminists, take back the night, the
moon, the stars, the atmosphere all the
way down to the streets in which we
gather. Walk together in pairs, en masse,
until we glide alone in safety, no longer
in fear of those who have stalked
the darkness in dominance for ages. The
night will no longer hide them from our
fierce desire to control our destiny.

Our fight is not women against men, but
good versus evil. Together, the feminists
of all genders, races, ages, ethnicities are
here. The night cannot save those who
would harm us.

Manhattan 1979: A Prose Poem

We walked into American Place Theatre, self-assured young lesbian feminist playwrights, radical co-founders of our own Actors Sorority with a musical comedy in the pockets of our overalls the theatre company wanted to discuss. One small problem—they wanted to talk us out of our all-woman cast. They thought men should play the male roles. We didn't budge, and we never went on to fortune or fame.

Instead we visited every women's theatre and dance company in Manhattan. We took the train to New Haven, where the Theatre of Light and Shadow was in rehearsal with our self-same musical comedy *The Clue in the Old Birdbath*. They had no problem with Nancy Drew's dad being played by a woman. We saw Spiderwoman Theatre Company and met the soon-to-be-famous Peggy Shaw and Lois Weaver. Then we saw their play, *An Evening of Disgusting Songs and Pukey Images*, again and again. We went to a women's music festival and had a serious discussion with June Millington. We lay on the floor of an all-white loft in SoHo and watched a rehearsal of a ballet about Clytemnestra and Orestes. We saw Paul Zaloom in a garage. Met JoAnne Akalaitis of Mabou Mines and saw their current show.

We had an uncomfortable evening at the Performing Garage where the audience could not leave without crossing the stage. We were miserable while watching a young woman actor fling her head back and forth hundreds of times, and have her naked torso bitten by two fully clothed men—

including Willem Dafoe. In protest I wrote a scathing letter to Spalding Gray. He wrote me. Ten pages. He had the actor write to tell me how she wasn't being abused, but was proud of her ability to fling her head. She didn't say she was proud to be bitten by Willem Dafoe. We young feminists returned to the Midwest, having had our Big Apple adventure, and lived to tell the tale.

Divided We Fall

Divided, we fall victim to our inherent
racism, our fear of differences, our
ignorance.

United, we can be allies for each
other, regardless of race, creed, color, or
gender. Lifting up our sisters, our
brothers, elevates us all, as if on a
rising tide.

Let us be among the first to speak
up, speak out against wrongs, when we
see them, hear about them, and
finally recognize them.

Let us join in learning more about
all others who occupy this world with
me and you. Let's help each other be
the love that unites us all.

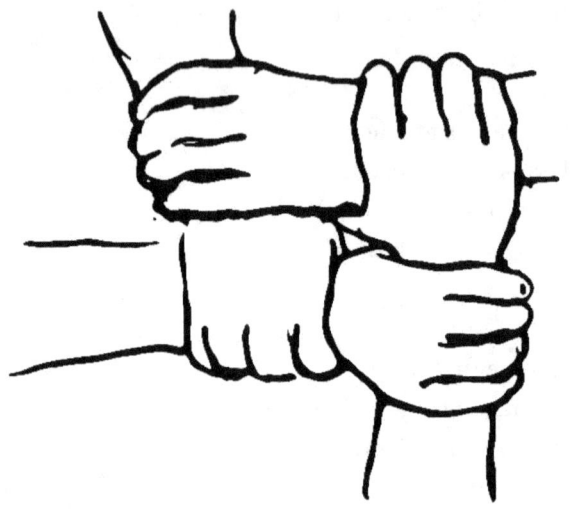

WAR
AND PEACE

Foreboding

Presentiment is that long shadow on the lawn
Indicative that suns go down;
The notice to the startled grass
That darkness is about to pass.
~Emily Dickinson

Something is about to happen. It's as if
someone walked on my grave.

My grandma used to say that. The
shadow that flows past in my peripheral

vision, the feeling that gathers in
a cloud of smoke at my ankles.

There is no escaping the foreboding, and
no way to stop the cause.

Hiroshima Stories

1. He reaches to pull her into the
boat by her arm. Her skin comes
off like an elbow-length glove.

2. The morning sky is clear, the day will be
hot and dry. A perfect morning for dropping
Little Boy. His plane is *Enola Gay*, named for his
Mom back in Quincy.

3. For its safety, she puts her sewing machine in the concrete
basin filled with water. She is watching her neighbor when
the world flashes white and she flies through the air
pursued by a shower of timber and tiles.

4. At the Red Cross Hospital one doctor is uninjured. He
attends ten thousand patients for more than three days
with only one hour's sleep, as thousands die and pile up.

A-Bomb

The lucky ones were those who never
even saw the flash. They were vaporized
instantly, most leaving nothing behind,

not even a shadow. Those who thought
they were lucky as they ran through the
day assisting others, apologizing for being

alive, uninjured, seeing horrors we can't
even imagine today, those people were
dying on the inside: cell by cell. Radiation

sickness was already at work.
The many men and few women who
worked so hard and fast to create this

"gadget" meant to end the war to end all
wars now saw not only the end of World
War Two, but what annihilation the bomb had wrought.

Many then became as dedicated to peace
as they had been to creating the bomb. In
a perfect world, no nuclear weapon

will ever be released in this or any universe again.
At the first test of this power, the man whose work
allowed confirmation of Einstein's mass-energy concept
said, "Now we are all sons of bitches."

And began his dedication to the end of testing.

Shadows of War

One morning on the way to work at my job
in downtown Portland, Oregon, I emerged
from the bus and saw outlines
of bodies on the sidewalks.

Had there been a mass murder in the night?
Where was the crime scene tape? Why were
people scurrying to their offices as though
nothing had happened?

That August morning was not unlike
the day one single bomb destroyed Hiroshima.
Cloud cover was light. The air was warm. People
in Hiroshima were at school or at work or at

home. They were on the streets headed out to
shop for food, or visit family, or to take a walk.

Above them, a single plane flew. On the ground
a man recognized it as being from the United
States. He knew Japanese planes didn't fly that high.

Enola Gay loosed that one explosive. The one
named *Little Boy* fell forty-three seconds before
activation. Men on the plane had time to
believe the bomb was a dud. The plane flew

more than eleven miles before the
shock waves hit. And it kept flying.
On the ground, people eleven miles from
ground zero survived the initial blast.

Most people, most life, most of the buildings
were incinerated where they stood. The radius of
total destruction was about one mile.

The resulting fires burned
about four and a half square miles.
In the first minutes after the blast,
vaporized humans left only

outlines of their bodies.

August 1985 I was reminded of that day
by the death shadows a group of peace activists left
to commemorate the fortieth anniversary.

More than thirty years have passed since
hundreds of people went out in the night
to paint thousands of death shadows on the
streets and pavements of cities across the USA.

And yet, the threat of nuclear war looms
again. Leaders with short tempers and big
arsenals grumble and threaten to unleash
fire and fury, to destroy nations.

They call each Rocket Man and Dotard.
Who will laugh at their feeble jokes
when we are reduced to mere
shadows of our former selves?

White Sands

The white sands of Alamogordo drew scientists
to them as if the sands' glory existed at the edge of
a jade green sea where people could wade
in warm waters, waves lapping at their ankles.

White sands inspired the scientists' over-active brains
to dream up massive weapons whose damage
they could never imagine.

The scientists and their lackeys donned
dark glasses as though going to the beach
for a picnic, lying on their bellies on the strand.

Instead of watching a sunset, they opened their
mouths in awe at the size of the mushroom
clouds the bombs created. They filmed.

The cloud, themselves, houses, pigs, and the
mannequin families, they documented every
aspect. The white sands absorbed it all

in silence. Even now the sands tell secrets
only in radioactive beeps.

Black Gold

The United States is dependent
on oil. Petroleum is extracted
from the earth in the millions of
gallons every day.

It fuels the economy as it
powers our vehicles, warms
our homes, ignites the fires
of war.

Black gold spews or is drawn
out of the depths of our planet
and put to use for our comfort
and convenience.

Countries are willing to send
troops to kill and die for this
precious commodity.

More precious than human life?
Dearer to us than forests and
animals and birds? More
important than our oceans?

The US has already warred
with Iraq. May soon attack
Iran. How long until the
conflict with Saudi Arabia?

There is even more oil
in Venezuela. Most oil
reserves are in Canada.
Blood will flow like oil.

Nine-Eleven

This year I heard the words
"Never forget" in a different way.

Was it always intended we "remember
9/11" by hating immigrants

hating Muslims, hating and hating?

No. My heart cries as I remember
the beautiful morning the planes

hit the towers, hit the Pentagon,
crashed in a field in Pennsylvania.

I remember the nearly three thousand
people who died on that day, the many

more who perished later from illness
disease, and injuries related to the attack.

I remember how terrified we were.
As intended. The sound of planes

overhead, even thousands of miles
from the East Coast, struck terror

on the days following. We must not
let terror win, we said.

We went on. And we promised
to never forget. I remember.

Even the Evil Deserve to Rest in Peace

I checked my phone for messages and saw the text alert from The New York Times: *The White House says bin Laden has been killed.* Television waits for almost an hour for the official announcement.

President Obama looks excited, as if he can barely contain himself. Stumbles over two or three words in his short announcement. He's reading every word. I'm watching him closer than I ever have before. What am I looking for? I listen for reassurance that they got the right man. I get it.

They've known bin Laden's location for nine months. They've zeroed in for the past week. I keep thinking about the president out golfing nine holes earlier in the day. What were his thoughts? What was his score? What is Michelle thinking as she watches this? *Is* she watching this? Does she hide the children from him when he returns, bubbling over with testosterone?

For he is, isn't he? That's what is seeping from the television. I can feel it pulsing through the fiber optics as though it were pumping through veins.

Today I learn that people fled to the White House to wave flags, filled the streets of New York City to sing the national anthem. Here on my street all was quiet, just as in my house.

All night, I thought about the phrase: we have his body. We are in possession of bin Laden's body. We will dispose of his body. Today I read that "we buried him at sea."

I picture his head in a refrigerator somewhere. His hands kept for proof of identity. Let it be true that we feel nothing after death. Osama bin Laden, rest in peace.

Poem to 45: you don't deserve a capital Y.

you are a yellow-bellied, orange-skinned, cold-blooded, cold-hearted, blue-balled, red-baiting, anti-Semitic, green-eyed toddler eager to pull the wings off our planet in order to line your shallow pockets with gold.

you ignore the cries of the hungry, the houseless, the disabled, the poor, the elderly, the people who work for a living, the people who voted for your ass.

you ignore ethics, you ignore morals, you ignore history. you ignore the Constitution, the judicial system, and the law. your bankrupt past informs your bankrupt soul. you cut funding for education, for the arts, for healthcare, but you blow up Syria and Afghanistan to justify your increase in military spending.

We see you hiding behind your agenda as you golf every weekend at the castle while we're forced to rent golf carts for the Secret Service to watch you entertain the minions who can afford an annual fee of two hundred thousand dollars to be your yes men.

you don't deserve to breathe the black air inhaled by the coal miners you deceived. If you ever need health care, you deserve the same as those who are denied due to pre-existing conditions or inability to pay.

When you've bullied Queen Elizabeth II into giving you a ride in her gold carriage, its wheels should fall off as an indicator of what will happen to your presidency when your constituents wake the hell up. Dawn is coming. Some of us have been up all night waiting for the alarm to go off.

Margaret Nin* to Her Husband Johann Faust, 1597

When the lantern shattered and took out my
eye, I bore up with good will. The injury gave me no
more pain than to bear our two great sons who

are with you now and will help you run the
farm. When Herr Weitz claimed I caused his
horse to jump the stall and become ill, and

Frau Henses said she lost her eye because my
eye was gone and took hers as a companion,
others followed and swore it was true, I am

a witch, a consort of the devil. They said I did
dance with Lucifer and lie with him
in the meadow, but Hans I have never lain

with anyone but you, and could not say I had.
I send my tongue to you, as I will
not come back, whole or otherwise.

They ripped my tongue from me because I would not lie.
Now I can never speak again. Tonight
after the lights are out, I will tie

my bed sheets together and fling them over
the rafter. Never more will I see you.
Take good care of little Hans.

GGGGGGGreat-grandmother of the poet, Sandra de Helen

Time Out for Peace

Only those who have given of
themselves to nurture and raise
others to know the meaning and
value of self-sacrifice. Therefore

Let all nurturers of all children
of all countries of the world
appoint a council of nurturers/
mothers to meet for one purpose:
to nurture the world. To put an

end to all war. To ensure our
mother, the Earth, lives without
harm caused by humans. To
promote peace, and above all
harmony. To tame all feelings
of harm and revenge. To make
known the happiness of unity.

Let them pack lunches for all
of us, and let us spread our
blankets around the world. Let
us sit together in time out until
we embrace the lesson of
peace.

Sandra de Helen

THE PERSONAL IS POLITICAL

Schlitz! A Drinking Song

Here's to the beers that saddened my life
Cheers to the tears I cried
Fears of the raging, the beatings, the strife
Resentments 'til the day she died.

You're not an alcoholic if you drink only beer
It's never a hangover, only a head
If you don't like it, you can get out of here
Never mind my pals haunting your bed.

Drinking is fun, beer is for life!
Taverns are better than home.
Birthdays, holidays, every dog and her wife
Drink Schlitz, and dance down your bones.

We love that brown logo! Who needs food or new shoes?
Buy Schlitz and have friends by the score!
Even by the case, beer is not really booze
Stanch the hunger and angst. Simply buy more!

More beer, more Schlitz, more friends at the door
More anger, more trauma, who cares?
Your friends know you're a good mother at core
Get drunk, have fun, who said life was fair?

Disney Revolution

The first movie I saw in color was
Bambi, also the first movie to make me
cry. The screen and my mother stand
tall in my memory, the colors are clear
as tears, though not so glaringly bright
as the colors of today. I was five and
small for my age, though I cried big tears
when Bambi's mother was shot by the
hunter.

My father hunted, but never for big
game like deer. He bagged squirrels or rabbits
for our suppers. Mom couldn't kill a
chicken. So if Dad didn't shoot it or
catch it in the river, we had beans or
eggs.

I laughed at Flower the skunk and
Thumper the rabbit as they taught
baby Bambi the ropes. After Bambi's
mother was shot, after I dried my tears
with the hanky Mom handed me from
her purse, all the way home I thought
about the hunter.

The next night at supper as I picked
up my rabbit leg, I asked, is this the
same thing as a real rabbit? Like
Thumper? The answer meant I could
never look at Dad the same way again.
Or eat another piece of rabbit.

Vegetarian Now

The first time I gave up
meat, fish and chicken
I lasted twelve years.

What brought me crashing down was
barbecue. Ginny's barbecued chicken.
I resisted the first time.

Even the second and third. Finally gave
in, then went whole hog. Really.

Bacon, ribs, pork chops,
tenderloin, everything but
pickled pigs' feet and head cheese.

Beef too. Hamburgers anyway.
Chicken, chicken, chicken. Until
Dalai Lama came to town.

He begged KFC to stop using
chickens that were having their
beaks removed before being
killed. KFC refused.

I stopped eating chicken. Forever.
I ate hamburgers though. Organic
free range beef. And pork.

Then I drove through Missouri
to Iowa taking pictures of barns
along the way.

Stopped on Jesse James Road.
An entire herd of steers,
organic free-range beef cattle,

ran after me, bawling. Calling
me out. Begging me to free them.
I left, haunted.

Two days later, I drove back to see them.
They were all gone. All but two. Two
kept for family meals.

Me: Vegetarian again since
April 21, 2008.

Rabbit

Every month, first day of the month,
first thing out of my mouth are the words
rabbit, rabbit, rabbit.

An old superstition, guaranteed to bring me
good luck all month long. Has it ever worked?
An entire month not of good luck, but of
no bad luck?

I didn't grow up with this superstition. Instead
we didn't throw hats on the bed, or sing at the
table. We knocked on wood, refused to step
on cracks, lest we break our mother's back.

Except when I was really, really mad at Mom.
Then I stepped on every crack I could find.
All the way to school.

I wished on first stars. I wished when I
blew out birthday candles. I wished my
Dad was alive. I wished Mom wouldn't drink.

Grandma warned me to stop wishing
my life away. To live it instead. To be
grateful for what I had.

I was grateful when I was able to stop
eating rabbits. Now every month I
speak to them in gratitude. Rabbit,
rabbit, rabbit.

Sole/Soul

Once I fit under the sole of
anyone's shoe, so small it was
impossible to see the sky

except in glimpses as a boot
or slipper or high heel lifted in its step
on her way to the altar to marry

another step-father. Once I
dreamed my life from ridges of
rubber tread seeing streams

of sunlight as paths to a better
life in the land of Someday,
Somewhere.

My soul knew more than I did
and kept my dreams alive while
I did push-ups

in the breast of the shoe
gaining strength to find my way
up and over.

Diving In

High Banks belonged to the
boys. No girls allowed. Ever.

Males swung on a rope, far
out over the river. Jumped,

whooped, swam freely. I stood
on the far side, filled with feelings.

Envy first, then sadness for
being excluded. Next came
anger. And the question: Why?

Don, Dwayne, Kansas and
I hung out together, played

in the woods. Threw knives at
my "man" in the basement.

I drew him on the wall of the
newly built closet, became

expert at getting him right in
the eye. The boys and I were
close.

Yet there they were, swimming
and laughing, having
too much fun. Without me.

On the other side of the bridge
were the girls and shallow water.

No swing, only boring moms
with their beer and gossip.

I wanted to dive in the waters
of High Banks.

I longed to swim like a girl in
the boys club.

The Right Foundation

Every day when I carried
the money drawer to the
drive-up window
you waited for a quick feel.

I was in training.
I was going to be
a real bank teller
a man's job.

If I complained
I would lose my chance.
I'd seen what happened
behind the teller windows
to Frankie, the other
woman teller, Vern's
hand on her ass.

You slid your hand
under my dress
above the stocking
reaching for the
sweet spot.

I needed this job.
I deserved this job.

We were required
to wear stockings,

dresses or skirts,
slips, girdles, not
too much jewelry.

I went shopping.
I bought a new girdle.
A rubber Playtex
to wear over panties.

Two pairs of panties.
And a sanitary pad.
Every day of the month.

When you frowned, I
shrugged.
Playtex was the
right foundation.

Be a Hairy Woman

Put your left hand back at your
waist and fondle the locks of your flowing
blond hair at ages eight, sixteen
and twenty-four.

Your mother starts a trend when you are eight.
Chopping off your braids in anger, and not allowing
another haircut until you are sixteen.

The pattern is set. You cut it above the
ears on your birthday. Wear it short
three years then let it grow to your
beltline.

At twenty-four it seems too heavy. Outdated.
Off it goes. For three years. And then you let it
stream over your shoulders and down your
back once again.

At thirty-three you come out and
buzz-cut your hair. Shocker.
By age sixty you've been following the pattern
all your life. You cut it again.

Then again from waist-length to above the ears
at seventy-one. Let it grow until it
brushes mid-back. Three years go by, and
we all know what happens next.

Abundance

Resisting consumption becomes me
—as well as my living space.
Minimalism has its place
it seems, in my home. See?

The walls are not without art
the floors are not bare
in fact, the rugs I care
for are Turkish at heart.

I work from my chair, legs
resting on an Eames' ottoman
my laptop as busy as I am
until I prepare to exit

my granny flat. Happy I
sprung for the glass door
that always presents more
bounty for my happy eyes.

Less is the key here
I still have too much
I find myself clutching
my favorite cashmere,

books, plants, blue jeans,
coats, jackets, too keen
on my favorites, I fear.

Minimalism has its place,
yes. But maybe not here
after all. Maybe my place
is too small a space.

I'll aim for compact,
tidy, neat, and clean.
An uncluttered routine,
that's my contract.

Two hundred square feet.
One person, one cat
Six jackets, one hat
Twelve dresses, complete

half my closet, a dresser
that's all, no mess here
I promise, replete.

Politics and Betrayal

We were best friends. We were also
feminists. But drugs were involved

and low self-esteem. Also one of us
had a higher sex drive than the other.
Me, I did.

That drive, combined with drugs and
alcohol, led me to make decisions I regret.
One of them was the betrayal of my

best friend. For months, she, her
husband, our friends and I fought
side by side against the war, and

to take over the Democratic party of
Alaska. We were the Ad Hoc group
of young people who went door to
door across the state,

organizing the voters, capturing one
precinct at a time, and on the night
of the elections, we met at our headquarters

for an all-night party. We drank
the Kool-Aid. Tripping on acid, high
on winning, when her husband

embraced me on the stairs, I pulled him
to me as if he were starving and I was the
only sustenance.

No thought of my best friend, not even a nod
to feminism, barely a care as to privacy.

She didn't learn of that night's betrayal until they
divorced years later. He found a way to hurt her more
by naming me.

Point/Counterpoint

With passion, we discussed #ferguson, #blacklivesmatter, and #ericgarner, using only interpretive dance, and Esther Williams-type swimming. I wore black tights and leotard, you wore a sapphire blue tank suit.

Sometimes, it was difficult to understand the other's point, so we took a moment to breathe, then watched carefully.

Splashes of my perspiration dripped in counterpoint to your splashless kicks in the pool.

Later we ate lunch. Later still, we raised our arms for a silent moment, and used them to hug.

The Joys of Working

Lethargy sets in about this time
every month. My toes refuse to
pick themselves up off the ground

and I drag them forward into tomorrow
unwillingly, scraping off last week's
nail enamel onto the hardwood floors

push myself up the stairs as I go to bed
early. After a mere thirteen hours sleep
of the dead, five alarms manage

one eyelid open enough to pull
the rest of my body off the edge
onto the floor.

I roll downstairs, don my waiting
uniform and apron, tie on my
shoes, eat a day-old bagel from

yesterday's plate, crawl into my
car and burn gasoline driving to
Flo's Diner because

today is payday, and surely to Pete
I can stand one more day.

The Duel

I took my power in my hand.
And went against the world;
'T was not so much as David had,
But I was twice as bold.
I aimed my pebble, but myself
Was all the one that fell.
Was it Goliath was too large,
Or only I too small?
~Emily Dickinson

Armed only with optimism
I went out in to the world, a
wife large with child at the
age of fifteen.

I aimed my pebble, and
Patriarchy fell. Not all the way
over, never all the way
down, but optimism is
the ultimate weapon.

I am still here. Patriarchy is
on life support.

Here, Bury This

Here is a word I'm never going to
use. I tried back in the seventies when
Germaine Greer said it was the word
all feminists should embrace.

I tried again in the eighties
when I moved to the
Pacific Northwest where
women were rugged and unafraid
to face their nether regions
without euphemisms.

Then in the nineties I went to Ireland
and heard men call each other by that name
and suddenly I was confused.

How could I reclaim a name I had never used
that was being tossed around like a rugby ball?

Twenty years later my poetry group
debates use of the c word versus
the two v words and as much as I love all the

cunt poems I've read, I'm never
going to say that word out loud.

Can You Hear Me Now?

Some artists are reluctant to add their
names to their work. Others paint
nothing but. Over and over and over

again they head out into the night to
spray paint their assumed names on
walls, posts, signs, doors, floors, and

trains. Florid, floral, balloons made of
letters, old school, or modern styles,
names and names and names.

Where are the slogans, the protests, the
wry humor? One or two lone souls dare
to speak their minds. Gone are the days

of graffitied stop signs with the added words
"the war" or "rape" or the Keep Off the Grass
signs with stenciled marijuana plants. Have

the artists grown lazy? Or apathetic? No
longer content with "Kilroy was here," each
adds their own pseudonym for our amusement.

Girls graffiti their hair, everyone gets tattoos.
No dumpster, trash can, or sign is safe from
the tattoos of street artists.

I was here. I was here.
I was here.
We all want to be heard.

To Each His Own

People in their bliss otherwise known as
ignorance, sometimes speak as if people

like me are different from people like
them. Making remarks like: it's a

preference, a lifestyle, a choice,
a passing phase. If these people

are your parents they hope
you will grow out of it.

Change your mind, the way you
change your hairdo. Start hanging

with a different set and suddenly
you will like boys. But then

you never do and you grow up
to hear your neighbors say "to each his own."

CELEBRITY POLITICS

Emancipation

No rack can torture me,
My soul's at liberty
Behind this mortal bone
There knits a bolder one
You cannot prick with saw,
Nor rend with scimitar.
Two bodies therefore be;
Bind one, and one will flee . . .
~Emily Dickinson

Born. Assigned gender: male.
Given a boy's name, played boy's
games, played them so well he
became an Olympian. A hero,
a champion.

Lived a life in the limelight.
Married a woman, had children.
Daughters. Famous daughters.
Grandchildren. Television, cameras,
interviews, reality, all probing,
all delving, all watching, wondering
who is this man and why is he
changing?
right before our eyes . . .

All those years, a cocoon. Behind that
mortal bone, knitted a bolder one.
Behold the new one. Once Bruce,
now Caitlyn Jenner.

A Message to Gloria Steinem

"This is what forty looks like," you proclaimed.
I copied you ten years later by performing a
personal one-woman show for fifty of my
friends.

Beautiful woman, head full of brains, you
led me not into temptation, but into a
life of fully lived feminism. Of activism,
of writing.

MS magazine rejected me so many times, I
gave up submitting.
You said "A woman without a man is like
a fish without a bicycle." I lived without
men and kept my bicycle. I didn't give up
writing.

Now you are eighty, and I, as always, am
ten years behind.

This year you will continue to light the
way, and I will follow.

Elegy for Lanford Wilson

Mr. Wilson, I never met you although
I saw you in person across the room

here in Portland when I came to see
your play, which one it doesn't matter

I've seen or read them all. You were
born a few miles from my own place

of birth, you too were born gay in a
place and time where that made us

outsiders as much as our being writers
made us odd. You inspired me with

your work, your life, your courage to
love your characters, to show the

world—as did Tennessee Williams,
who once lived in St. Louis—to show

people haven't changed a damn bit.
We can recognize everyone.

Hef, circa 2012

He set out to do something for the
good of man: create a magazine featuring
mammillae for the intellectual and urbane

gentleman who associated sex with the
girl next door. He became the iconic
image of his targeted reader: playboy

with silk smoking jacket, pipe, surrounded by
bunnies of astounding beauty. Over
time Hef developed a mammoth-size

case of Mammonism* as he developed
key-clubs, mansions, hotels, television
shows, resorts, modeling agencies, books,

circulations of more than a million copies
of *Playboy* per issue. At his company's
peak, the magazine was selling over twelve
million copies each month and Hef lay

on a circular bed inside a DC-30 jet with
sixteen guests circling the globe. Today he is in
silk pajamas, still living his fantasies

with young women and blue pills. He is
eighty-six years old.

**Mammonism, n. the greedy pursuit of capitalism*

Goodbye, Hugh. Seriously

>after Judy Grahn's *I Have Come to Claim Marilyn Monroe's Body*

I have come to claim Hugh Hefner's body
for the sake of all women. I want those long
hard bones. I will carry them in my pockets,

spread them on a table for women to ogle.
He wanted so badly to be taken seriously.
Hugh Hefner, self-styled protagonist for racial

equality and gay rights, proclaimed himself
the instigator of the sexual revolution. But women
looked better in corsets and high heels,

according to Hef. He seriously stuck a tail on them.
Playmates had more fun at his orgies if they were doped up
with Quaaludes. They took them along

with the money in exchange for their bodies. Life in the
Playboy mansion was a paradise. For him.
He took himself so seriously.

For the women who were playfully called bunnies,
symbol of fertility, the mansion was a prison.
But the satin prison uniforms with their nipped-in waist
lines,

their too-low necklines, and their too-high thigh lines,
were cute. Seriously.
Hugh Hefner obsessed about Marilyn Monroe.

Young Hugh wanted to see her naked so badly, he spent
five hundred dollars for the rights to her photograph
for the cover of his new magazine. After her death, he bought
the crypt next to Marilyn's. Now his dead body lies beside
hers.

This is serious.
Hugh Hefner will spend eternity next to her because
he made his fortune off pictures of women.

Marilyn would run, if she could.
She doesn't deserve to lie next to his
rotting corpse. He should be the one to leave.

For the sake
of all women,
I am here to take him away.

I have come to claim Hugh Hefner's body. I will put it in a
plain brown wrapper and hide it in a drawer. When I die,
my heirs will toss him into the trash.

POET WARRIORS
AT WORK

Poet Warriors

When the barometric pressure drops, hunters know the animals will be on the move, anglers know to look for fish in certain places they wouldn't otherwise hide. Cows, goats, sheep and dogs will stir, run, bark, moo or baa when an earthquake is about to hit.

When fascism is on the rise, resistors rise as well. When you notice the poets getting rowdy, you know something big is happening. Revolution is often in progress. War. People becoming warriors. Watch for the poets. Listen for the words that stir. Become a poet—if you're brave enough.

Deed

A deed knocks first at thought,
And then it knocks at will.
That is the manufacturing spot,
And will at home and well.
It then goes out an act,
Or is entombed so still
That only to the ear of God
Its doom is audible.
~Emily Dickinson

What deeds have we
suppressed, from fear or
indolence? Those thoughts
of bravery, courage, or
ambition. They knocked,
of course they did. But
where was our will? Our
drive to succeed? To
act?

We heard about the
injustices. We learned about
#Ferguson, #Eric Garner,
we know we need to
act. We tell ourselves we
wait for a leader.

The time has come to step
forward and let our hearts
show the way.

Disruptive/new self

Excuse me, I am not my old self.
After buying a small supply of Black Lives Matter
buttons to prove to all and sundry my
support as an ally, after celebrating
the Supreme Court decision in favor
of gay marriage, and watching our
president eulogize one of the nine black
people murdered in their church in one day,
I had hoped for a few minutes respite
from the terrorism against our own citizens.

But someone is burning black churches
all over the South. Their obstreperous
behavior is disturbing the balance
of my brain cells, tipping my normally
polite mannerisms over to the point
where instead of the butter knife I find
myself reaching for the nine-inch stabber. Rather
than answering texts with a pleasant
good afternoon, I am replying in all
CAPS and hashtags with
#WHOISBURNINGBLACKCHURCHES

If authorities can't find the answer by
morning, I may call for a gathering of
poet warriors across the country. We'll
don our ally buttons, link our arms in vast

chains and stand guard around the churches
until the authorities stop the burning, take
up the righteous cause themselves.

First Assignment: Extreme Heat Season

Temperature: hot enough to melt an
iPhone. I forgot my camera, was counting
on the smartphone as a backup.

Must rely on what wits remain despite the heat.
The strain on the city's power supply caused a blackout,
the entire area is in darkness.

No fans are turning, no air conditioners
or swamp coolers working. The people I
can make out in the steamy twilight

are sitting or leaning, waving pieces of
cardboard in front of their faces, not
moving otherwise. I force myself forward.

Only hospitals and a few government buildings
are lit by emergency generators. I can hear
them humming. The rest of the city appears to have
come to a near standstill.

Traffic lights are out. No one is enjoying
a bike ride or stroll. Police are standing on corners waiting
for someone on the other end of the radio

to tell them where to rush off to next. The officer
nearest me unscrews the top of her
water bottle and takes a long swallow.

I can hear her gulping over the sound of
cars honking four blocks over. Even the
horns sound less than crisp, as if they too
have softened in the oven of this city.

On the corner I spy a relic from times
past: a pay phone. I reach for the vandal-
resistant handset, expecting it to have been

cut from its cord, finding it intact, and
nestled in its cradle. One miracle leads to
the next until I found myself connected

to the news desk where I am able to submit
our report. To plead for relief for this
city's citizens, in whatever form available.

Will the Governor declare a state
of emergency? Will the National Guard
be sent in? Who will come to our aid?

I have every confidence someone will
be here soon, and things will return
to normal.

Civil Rights: Next Phase

I'm not black, but a storm is brewing inside
this ally. I'm ready and willing to join my fellow
humans in mass protest against racism. I may not be as
articulate as some, but my heart is full to
bursting with outrage.

Inside me is a revolutionary tiger.
I will accelerate and reveal it,
to fight the systemic racism of this country
founded on white supremacy.
Not by Proud Boys, or Patriot Prayer Men,
or whatever today's extremists call themselves
but by white people who believed they were supreme.
That all good things belong to white people
and only white people. All others
were deemed inferior.

As a white person, I may have suffered
discrimination for being poor, for being
LGBTQ, for being fat, or any number
of other reasons. But I have never
been black. I've never lost out
because of the color of my skin.
That is white privilege.

No one can tell me to be quiet any longer.
I will let flow my feelings about racism and hope
for an articulate stream as slick as grease.

Sandra de Helen

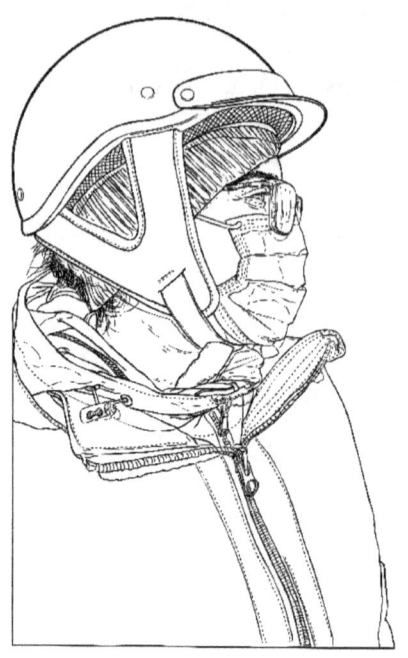

HOME ISOLATION DAYS

Day 66: A WWII Moon

A WWII moon shone –when I was born
ahead of the baby boomers, child
of parents who survived
the Great Depression, granddaughter
of a veteran of World War I.

I was born under a Scorpio moon,
full of dark secrets and intrigue.

I marched with the anti-war movement,
fought for the ERA, lost friends
to the scourge of AIDS.

I survived the No on 9 campaign
to drive out LGBTQ from Oregon,
marched in my pussy hat
with women grieving our loss of 2016.

I've protested racism, protested kids in cages.
Now I'm living under a pandemic moon,
walking for my health,
writing for my life.

Day 76: No End

No end in sight because people
are idiots.
Memorial Day people thronged
the parks and beaches
as if we had a vaccine
and they'd all been vaccinated.

There is no prevention other than quarantine
and no cure. Not yet.

The second wave may be a tsunami.

Meanwhile, I boil like an active volcano
every time I read even a bit of news.

The people protesting in Minneapolis
I understand. A police officer killed George Floyd
while his partner looked on. All on video.
I understand the urge to storm the castle
but a pandemic is raging. Even if I were there
even if George Floyd was my own kin
I'd hesitate to be close to other people.

These grieved, outraged citizens are not
the idiots of whom I despair.

The misguided fools who party at Lake of the Ozarks,
or hug in the street, as eight exercising young people
did two miles from here this afternoon,

these are the people who will spread Covid-19
without another thought.

They may not die if they're young and healthy,
but they will cause the deaths of thousands
who are not so fortunate.

Will people wise up when the death toll hits
one million? Two? Three?

I will rejoice in the fact my tomato plant
has flowers today. The hummingbirds
have plenty to eat. My daughter brought
home the groceries, and sprayed them
with bleach water. All is currently well.

•

Day 82: Can I Change?

Can I change hearts and minds? I'm trying.
I belong to a play reading group,
I run its website, I am on the board.

We are neither non-profit or for profit.
We do not depend on government grants
or conservative handouts.

We should stand up for human rights,
for justice, for diversity. We should support
the black lives matter movement.

I have requested our group to make a statement.
I would be the one to send out a newsletter
to update the website. No work for anyone else.

I'm getting pushback. And I am resisting.
We are a theatre arts group. If we don't support
diversity, justice, and human rights, we are a fraud.

I wasn't here when we were fighting for equal rights
to marriage. Did this group support that right?
Celebrate the win?

What did this group do during the Civil Rights Era?
It was formed in 1948, so it must have done something.
Doing nothing is political. Doing nothing does harm.

I am doing what I can.

Day 100: The First 100

First one hundred down.
How many hundred more
to go?

California had the most cases
of Covid 19 in a single day
yesterday.

But politicians say we have to reopen
because people just won't stay in.

Police and military have no trouble
using might to keep protestors down.

Economy the worst since the Great Depression.
But government help, what little there was
has to end.

Hospitals are near capacity in Arizona
and Texas.

Tulsa is set to erupt tomorrow
as Trump threatens protestors
this will be no Minneapolis.

Has he ordered the military
to shoot to kill protestors?

If I lived there, I would not protest.

I would stay home, stay safe
and let the Trumpsters infect each other.

Let the military stand around
with nothing to do. No one to shoot.

Living in isolation, I've noticed
it's not only my hair that is growing.
My anger has reached new depths,
and I cannot mask it.

Day 101: Tulsa Rally

Trump rallies 20,000 ignoramuses
in Tulsa. No masks, no social distancing
and many of his advance team
tested positive for Covid-19.

Is he trying to kill his followers?
Why not just give them the actual Kool-Aid?
It worked almost perfectly for Jim Jones.

Apparently, 80,000 other stupid heads
were unable to get tickets
for the rally of death.

There was a rally of life here in the park
this morning. Five rabbits came out
to say hello.

My neighbor's sago palm tree
is in bloom. What a sight.
The mourning doves and I
sang our praises.

Then I came home to sew.
The yellow dress progresses.

Day 110: Covid Dreams

Covid nightmares made a comeback
last night. Hours of dodging people
without masks coming too close.

I dreamed about a broom, too.
Time to sweep something clean?

In real life, I dream of moving house.
I long for Portland and proximity
to my family and friends there.

I imagine small social distance gatherings
in which I see loved ones' faces
above their masks.

We could sit ten feet apart
and still hear and see each other.
I'm sure it would be hard
not to hug. But the love would be palpable.

Lon Mabon, who tried to outlaw
gays in Oregon in the early 90s,
today said he'd rather be beheaded
than wear a mask.

Please make me President for a day.

Day 112: Happy July

Happy July. I wonder
whether this month
holds any happiness.

July is predicted to be
a banner month
for Covid 19.

The owner of our park
flaunts her bare face
as she shows her houses
to bare faced buyers.

I seethe in frustration
and rage.

I can let it all go
when I'm swimming
alone, safe, in the pool.

Day 115: Pointless Fireworks

Pointless fireworks.
There are so many other,
better, ways to celebrate.

In any case, I do not celebrate
Independence Day, because
like Frederick Douglas,
it has never included me.

All men are created equal.
Nope. And women are excluded.
On purpose. And never rectified.

Fireworks are an affront to the ears,
to the animals, birds, all wildlife.
They are a fire hazard. Dangerous.

The only time I ever held a Roman candle
I was ten and away from home.
It backfired into my eye.

A classmate lost half his arm
to fireworks when I was a kid.
Pets run away from home.
Every single 4th of July.

How did I spend my holiday?
Walking, writing, sewing.
Like any day. Today I made a hat.
A sunhat for my morning walks.

Tonight I'm grateful to live
in a relatively quiet place
where fireworks will be minimal
and my cat won't run away.

Day 120: Natural Hugs

Sadness hangs as heavy
as a summer storm,
over my head, in my heart.

When I was fourteen,
and again at twenty-one,
I carried on a love relationship
with an Air Force man.

Months of writing letters
of longing, filled with angst,
yearning, and day-to-day detritus.

The second time, we had occasional phone calls.
Hours of expensive long-distance
in which we languidly loved
the sound of our own voices.

This lockdown, this quarantine,
this imposed isolation
feels much the same.

Somewhere, at an unreachable distance
my loved ones go about their lives
in much the same way as I.
Masked, sanitized, careful,
and missing human touch.

Nature welcomes me every morning,
offers her bounty of birdsong,
rabbit tails, vegetation growing,
blooming, fruiting. But her arms
feel like breezes, not sweaty
human limbs, squeezing me tight.

How dare I pout, in the face
of a fluffy California towhee
who sings to me at my bedroom window?
Selfish being that I am, I'm only human.

Day 131: Living in the Now

What if there is no After Time?
Only Before Time and Now Time?
Because in the Now everyone is asking
when will this time end.

Everyone assumes there will be a vaccine.
But look at AIDS. Medication, yes.
No vaccine.

There was a time when everyone
who contracted AIDS was doomed
to death. Life insurance claims
were paid to the living-soon-to-die.

Then medication to allow living with AIDS
was developed, and people had to find
a way to live. To return to work,
in many cases.

Will we learn to live with Covid-19?
Nothing so simple as an annual flu shot,
but medication offering hope?
Lives altered by the virus, but life none-the-less?

I'm horrified by those who wish for a return
to "normal," to send children back to school
when there is no cure, no vaccine,
certain, though invisible, threat.

I make new masks to match the dresses
I've made in the past. I learn new sewing
tricks, go for my daily walks,
remember to be grateful for life.

Is this what they mean by living in the Now?

Day 174: I Believe

Looking forward, I believe I will survive
not only covid-19, but this lockdown
and the trump administration.

Looking forward, I believe we the people
will triumph by turning out to vote
in record numbers.

I believe we are stronger than evil
that is being thrown at us every day.
I believe that at root, people want to do good.

Maybe not every single person,
but the majority.

Germany survived a period of evil
greater than the one we are enduring.
The forces for good eventually came out in droves.

Looking forward, I believe in the human race
and its ability to evolve, to change
and lift individuals up until we are all lifted.

We are at a tipping point. Critical mass
must be attained, and I believe it will be.

Day 207: Fierce Feminist vs. Fly Catcher: Debate 2020

The fly took center stage
and sat there in the spotlight
for two minutes and three seconds.

Were the debates bugged?
By whom? The Russians?
Maybe RBG sent the fly?

Mr. Vice President, I'm speaking.
Not, may I speak, not excuse me.
Just a fact. I'm speaking, sit down
and shut up.

But two major questions went unanswered,
by both debaters. Will the Dems pack the court?
And what if trump refuses to leave?

I wish I knew. I'm guessing
both she and he were wishing the same.

OUTRO

Today's the Day

This is the day I go for it. Full out, full stop, no holding back. Plan A all the way. I'm straightening my shoulders, pulling in my chin, leading with my attitude.

I'm not asking for a favor, not pleading for a cause. I'm telling them what is what, and what I want.

I want full recognition, full rights under the constitution, full benefits under all laws, I demand to be seen, heard, and

felt. This is no dream where I punch them like a hankie wafting in a breeze. No. This is real life where

a fist landing on a body hurts both parties. Maybe not equally. But with pain.

They have to listen. They have to look into my eyes, my heart, my soul.

They will see themselves looking
back, reflected as the same person
the same soul as my own.

They have to. It's the only way.
I have no backup plan.

AUTHOR'S AFTERWORD

Art is political. All art is political, albeit not all art is *overtly* political. But saying nothing is still saying something. It might be saying to be quiet, we don't want to hear your viewpoints. It might be saying Beauty is what is important. And certainly, art can be political without being polemical. This collection of poetry was written to express my thoughts, opinions, and especially feelings, about what affects me as a woman, as a human being, as a member of the LGBTQ community. You may feel differently, have other thoughts, other opinions, other ideas about these same issues.

ABOUT THE POET

Sandra de Helen published her first poem at the age of fourteen. Her English teacher, Janice Wallace, submitted the poem to a teacher's magazine and surprised Sandra with a copy in print. The poem was about abortion, which was illegal at the time.

In her twenties, Sandra published a few poems in newspapers, which spurred her to take a Creative Writing Class at the local community college. The [male] professor professed she would never make a good poet because she didn't "write like a man." The next year she joined the women's movement and turned to writing plays.

Forty years later, she picked up Sage Cohen's book, *Writing the Life Poetic: An Invitation to Read and Write Poetry*, and resumed writing poems like a woman.

A long-time resident of Portland, Oregon, Sandra recently relocated to sunny California where she lives with her daughter and a very special cat.

ACKNOWLEDGMENTS

Thank you to all the poets in our Poem A Day group for your words regarding my daily poems.

Thank you to Dmae Roberts, who has supported my writing for many years, in person and on her radio show Stage and Studio.

Thank you to Judy Kahn, whose own poetry has inspired and rallied my spirit since I came out as a Lesbian in 1977.

Thank you to G. L. Morrison, lover of words, poet, and short fiction writer, for being a staunch fan of my work, and coming to my readings.

Thank you to the Portland Lesbian Writers Group whom I miss meeting with in person.

Thank you to the San Diego Writer's Ink writing group sponsored by the El Cajon Library. It was the first local writing group I sought out when I moved to California and has been a boon, especially during this pandemic.

Thank you to family and friends for always buying and reading my books. Your support means the world to me.

Special appreciation for my publisher, Lori L. Lake and Launch Point Press, for loving my words enough to put collections of my poetry into print. Not many publishers are willing to risk publishing poets unless the poets are already well-known. Kudos to you, Lori!

COPYRIGHT NOTES

Versions of these poems first appeared in the following publications:

"The Right Foundation," originally published in *All This Remains to be Discovered*, chapbook 2015.

"Poem to 45," originally published in *Quail Bell Magazine*, August 2017.

"Every Woman," originally published by *Artemis Journal*, June 2019.

Praise for Other Works by Sandra de Helen

Poetry

"These are fresh poems [in *Desire Returns for a Visit*] in every sense of the word. Flirty, audacious, original. A fresh take on Dickinson's love of women and words. A brazen exploration of the life cycle of love affairs. This book is an open-mouthed kiss to the reader. It will leave you breathless."
~G.L. Morrison, poet, lover of words, and short fiction writer

"[The poems in *All This Remains to be Discovered*] are a vulnerable, raw look at one's life with an undertone of tenderness and adult compassion and forgiveness. A very moving and worthwhile read."
~BuzzOregon

"I didn't need to read beyond the first line of the first poem to know I'd be loving this book."
~Lee Lynch, award-winning author of *Sweet Creek*

"I loved how honest and plain all the tales were [in *All This Remains to be Discovered*]. After reading this short book, I felt like I knew, intimately, every important person in the poet's life."
~Amazon.com Reader

Plays

"[The stageplay] *The Clue in the Old Birdbath* is proving to be catnip for the robust, unadorned, unescorted females in attendance. Unfolding is a musical demolition by Sandra de Helen and Kate Kasten of Carolyn Keene's nubile teen detective Nancy Drew, here renamed Tansy True. Here, adolescent literature's beacon of girlish pluck and ingenuity is rendered into a salty, torpedo-breasted assassin of male domination."
~Keith A. Joseph, Cleveland Scene

Novels

"*The Hounding* is . . . an interesting and well-developed mystery. I recommend it for any Holmes/Watson obsessives."
~Megan Casey, Lesbrary.com

"I wish I had half the plotting talent that Sandra de Helen has. [*Till Darkness Comes*] is such a terrific and totally satisfying book."
~Chelsea Cain, Thriller Writer, Humorist, and News Columnist

"If you are a lover of Sherlock Holmes, [*The Illustrious Client*] is a fun look at what might happen had the characters been women and in the present day. The books' titles are taken from Sherlock Holmes' own stories and this book is loosely based on the one of the same title. However, this is not just a

retelling of the Holmes stories. Ms. de Helen definitely makes it her own. The clues and red herrings as the pair solve the mystery are well placed. The plot was strong and interesting, and like a really good mystery, I couldn't figure out 'whodunnit' and was surprised by the reveal at the end."
~Long and Short Reviews.com

"[*The Hounding* is a] confident, meticulously detailed mystery that would have made Shirley [Comb's] pipe-smoking idol proud."
~Kirkus Reviews

"[*The Illustrious Client*] is certainly worth a read. With the author continuing to hone her talents, I am looking forward to the next one."
~Megan Casey, Lesbrary.com

www.ingramcontent.com/pod-product-compliance
Lightning Source LLC
Chambersburg PA
CBHW070116080526
44586CB00013B/1308